Culture of
Peace

Culture of Peace

David V. Edling
Series Editor

PEACEMAKER
MINISTRIES

HENDRICKSON
PUBLISHERS

Culture of Peace: The Peacemaking Church Series

©2003 Peacemaker® Ministries Published by Peacemaker Ministries

Hendrickson Publishers Marketing, LLC
P. O. Box 3473
Peabody, Massachusetts 01961-3473
www.hendrickson.com

ISBN 978-1-68307-175-4

First Printing Hendrickson Publishers Edition — May 2018

Printed in the United States of America

Contents

BIBLICAL PEACEMAKING

Building Real Relationships

Ken Sande and Gary Friesen

How had it come to this? For the first time in Mike's memory, Peter would not be joining the family for their annual Easter dinner. Mike thought back to the Easter ten years ago—just three days after their mother died—when in the midst of their grief, they resolved to gather as a family to celebrate their risen Lord. And then there was the Easter morning when they all woke to a raging blizzard. Even then, they had ventured through the snow and biting cold to come together for a warm family dinner.

Mike and Peter were not just brothers; for as long as Mike could remember, they had been best friends. They both loved the Lord and were active in the same church. Yet Mike couldn't break through his brother's increasing bitterness toward him.

How had it come to this? For fifteen years they had worked side by side in their father's construction business. Mike handled administration and marketing, and Peter oversaw the work crews. They earned the same salary and enjoyed a rewarding working relationship with their father.

Their relationship had begun to change about eighteen months ago when their father unexpectedly died. As directed by their father's will, Mike received the construction business and Peter received the family's vacation cabin. Their father's other assets were split evenly between them.

Everything seemed fine for a while. The two brothers worked together to take care of the estate duties, selling their father's house and sorting through his library. A few times Peter had expressed his concern to Mike about the difference in value between the successful business and the humble cabin, but Mike had found the conversations uncomfortable and always managed to change the subject. Looking back, he could see that Peter had begun to grow distant.

Peter finally showed his anger when Mike began to make changes in the construction business. From that point on, their ability to interact deteriorated rapidly. Now, several months later, they were communicating only through terse notes or third parties. Their wives, once close friends, barely spoke now. Their children preferred to steer clear of each other rather than to deal with the awkwardness of their parents' broken relationship. Both families still attended church, but it was apparent to everyone that they were estranged.

On a few occasions Mike had tried to talk to Peter, but it only made things worse. Peter seemed unable to respond without attacking

Mike's character, and he was apparently oblivious to his own selfishness and self-righteous anger. The men fell into a pattern of avoiding each other as much as possible.

So it had come to this—yesterday's brief, impersonal email: "Mike, we have made other plans for Easter. Peter."

Conflict is by no means a new thing. We see it as far back as the garden of Eden. One of the first conflicts of history—Adam and Eve versus God—had profound consequences. It threw our ancestors into ongoing patterns of conflict with one another. Worse yet, it separated them from the God with whom they had originally enjoyed an intimate, personal relationship.

Unfortunately, Adam's failure is our failure. Because the whole human race was represented by Adam, his sin has ongoing effects. It is with us to this day, rearing its destructive head in our lives on a daily basis, from our first breath on this planet to our last. It's in our blood, so to speak; we are sinners through and through. This is why conflict is inevitable, even among God's people.

But God has not deserted us in our sin and conflict. Because of his love for us, he sent his Son to earth to deliver us from our sin and save us from its eternal consequences (John 3:16). By taking our sins to the cross, Jesus paid for them and reconciled us with our heavenly Father (1 Pet. 3:18). Through faith in Christ's completed work, we will enjoy everlasting life with God in heaven, rather than facing eternal separation from him in hell.

Jesus' sacrifice also opened the way for us to handle problems on earth differently. By his grace, we can confess our sins and look to God for help in healing broken relationships. We can receive his power to change harmful attitudes and habits (1 John 1:9) and to live a life pleasing to him (Phil. 2:13). God's grace also enables us to resolve conflicts in a way that glorifies him and preserves precious relationships. The more we rely on his grace, the more effective we can be in living for God's glory as sinners who are also saints.

The hope this offers to those trapped in conflict is indescribable. Once we repent of our sins and confess them, our past sins become just that—past. God is a redeeming God who *wants* to forgive our sins and does so, wiping our slate clean. God delights in turning our ashes into beauty and our conflict into peace, and he is always able to help us change our ways so that we are swept up more and more into his wonderful plan for our lives (2 Pet. 1:3–4).

God wants his love for us to be reflected in our love for one another (John 13:34–35). Therefore, he wants us to resolve our conflicts with one another in a way that blesses those around us and strengthens our relationships (John 17:23). But he does not merely tell us that we *should* make peace with each other. He also graciously provides us with thorough instructions on *how* to resolve conflict. In addition to this, he promises to guide and enable us as we put these principles into practice.

Conflict Provides Opportunities

To a person who likes to escape from problems, conflict can appear to be either an inconvenience to be ignored or a frightful situation to avoid. And to someone who has a habit of attacking, it appears to be a chance for selfish gain. But to a Christian who wants to resolve differences through peacemaking, conflict is radically different. It is an opportunity to draw attention to the presence and power of God.

This is what the apostle Paul taught the troubled Christians in Corinth when they struggled with religious, dietary, legal, and family disputes:

> So whether you eat or drink or whatever you do, do it all for the glory of God. Do not cause anyone to stumble, whether Jews, Greeks or the church of God—even as I try to please

everybody in every way. For I am not seeking
my own good but the good of many, so that
they may be saved. Follow my example, as I
follow the example of Christ. (1 Cor. 10:31–11:1)

This passage reveals that *Paul viewed conflict as an opportunity to glorify God, to serve
other people, and to grow to be like Christ.* In
today's self-absorbed world, this perspective
sounds radical—even naive and foolish. But this
approach to conflict can be highly effective, and
it always pleases God.

Glorifying God is the highest calling of a
Christian. When we are in the midst of conflict,
we have an opportunity to show what Jesus has
done for us, and to reflect the love and kindness
of Christ in the way we treat those who have
wronged us. The more Jesus' grace and character
are revealed in us, the more God is honored and
praised (1 Pet. 2:12).

Conflict also provides an opportunity to
serve our neighbor by "seeking his good."[1] We
are to love our neighbors as ourselves, even if
they are disappointing or mistreating us (Luke
6:27–28). This is especially true with those who
are closest to us. When we are in a conflict, we

---

1. Scripture uses the term "neighbor" to describe
anyone with whom we have a relationship or with
whom God brings us into relationship.

can bless them by carrying their burdens, being a good example, correcting them in a loving and helpful way, and forgiving them as God has forgiven us (Eph. 4:32). Such service blesses those around us and honors God.

The third opportunity in a conflict is growing to be more like Christ (Rom. 8:28–29). Conflict offers us an ideal opportunity to strengthen and develop our character, whether by showing us where we need to grow or by requiring us to practice love and forgiveness in the face of irritation and frustration.

These three opportunities open the way to a biblical pattern for responding to conflict called the **Four G's**:

- **G**lorify God
- **G**et the log out of your own eye
- **G**ently restore
- **G**o and be reconciled

Let's consider each of these steps further.

Glorify God

Our God is a great and holy God, and our greatest privilege in life is to bring him glory. One of the most significant ways we can bring

honor and praise to God is by continually remembering what he did for us through his Son.
Jesus' death on the cross stands for all time as
the prime example of grace and mercy; it is lit-
erally our salvation from never-ending agony in
hell and our invitation to a relationship with our
heavenly Father. When we make Christ's work
on the cross central in our lives, our lives become
beautiful in his sight.

In addition to being the key to the Christian life, remembering what Christ has done for
us is the key to glorifying God through conflict.
This memory inspires us to trust God, not ourselves, for the results in any conflict (Ps. 56). It
motivates us to obey his commands (John 14:15),
and it helps us to imitate the character of Christ
as we interact with those around us (Eph. 5:1;
Phil. 2:5–8). Trusting, obeying, and imitating
Christ are essential to responding to conflict in
a God-pleasing way. When we live like this, we
glorify our gracious and loving God.

Trusting, obeying, and imitating Christ in
conflict brings other benefits as well. To begin
with, these godly habits help us set our mind on
the things of God. When we think about our relationship with our loving Father, we will find it
easier to resist sinful urges (pride, control, bitterness, and so on) and to respond in love and
obedience to God. Our emotions—which can

often be our worst enemy—are less controlling when we focus on God, and we are less inclined to give in to them.

Another benefit is that we become less dependent on results and on other people's behavior. Although someone may respond negatively or ignore our peacemaking efforts, we can be content and at peace knowing that we have trusted and obeyed God (Rom. 12:18). We can thus persevere even through the most difficult circumstances.

Practically speaking, we can focus our eyes on Jesus by asking ourselves one central question during any kind of conflict: "How can I please and honor God in this situation?" This was the thought on Jesus' mind during his earthly ministry (John 5:30; 8:29), and it should be on ours as well, especially when we are involved in conflict.

What would happen if Mike and Peter sought to glorify God in their conflict?

Instead of acting out of fear, self-interest, or bitterness, both Mike and Peter would look for ways to please and honor God. Rather than trying to control each other or their situations, they would choose to imitate God by purposefully reflecting his love and character in the days ahead. With their priorities focused on what brings God glory, each brother would be able to examine his own contribution to this painful conflict more objectively. Each would be motivated to reach out to the other in love, trusting God and being content regardless of the response.

Get the Log Out of Your Own Eye

Rarely, if ever, are we entirely innocent of wrongdoing in any conflict. Thus, after focusing on God, our next focus in conflict should be on ourselves—not to defend our actions or develop a plan to "win" the conflict, but to examine ourselves and confess our own sins. This is not a natural response to conflict. We are typically inclined to blame others and focus on their wrongs. But Jesus teaches us to take a radically different approach. In Matthew 7:5 he commands, "You hypocrite, first take the plank out of your own eye, and then you will see clearly to remove the speck from your brother's eye."

If we deal with conflict in this way, God will graciously help us to recognize our weaknesses and to depend more on his grace, wisdom, and power. He will also use conflict to show us our sinful habits and attitudes and help us to change. Prominent among the habits and attitudes we have seen in our own lives are pride, a tendency to put on appearances, an unwillingness to forgive, and a critical tongue. Conflict has a way of bringing these sins to the surface, giving us the opportunity to confess them to our forgiving God.

"Getting the logs out" of our own eyes can also speed up the resolution of a conflict. First, this examination enables us more quickly to face our contribution to a dispute. If we have been the main cause of a conflict, we can do a lot to resolve it simply by confessing our role and asking for forgiveness.

Second, even in a conflict where we do not believe we are the primary cause, we probably have played some role in making it worse. If we do not first take responsibility for what we have done, it will be difficult, if not impossible, to get the other person to deal with his or her part in the conflict.

Finally, confessing our own sins—and taking steps to change our behavior—may have a softening effect on our opponent. It may encourage him to listen to us more openly and even follow our example in facing his own contribution to the problem.

There are two basic types of logs that we need to confess (called "planks" in some versions of the Bible). One has to do with our attitudes, especially critical, negative, or oversensitive attitudes that fan the flames of a conflict.

The second log involves words and actions. Some of the things we say make conflict worse. These hurtful words feed a conflict rather than starve it; they include grumbling or complaining, gossip, unloving criticism, and lies or exaggerations of the truth to strengthen our position. Our actions also play a role in worsening conflict. These include doing things we should not do or failing to do things we ought to do, such as being lazy, not fulfilling our responsibilities, failing to keep commitments, resisting godly advice, or withholding mercy and forgiveness.

As God helps us to see our sins, we can get the logs out of our eyes by making a thorough confession. One way to do this is to follow the pattern laid out in the **Seven A's of Confession**:

ADDRESS everyone involved (all those whom you affected).

AVOID "if," "but," and "maybe." (Do not try to excuse your wrongs.)

ADMIT specifically (both attitudes and actions).

ACKNOWLEDGE the hurt. (Express sorrow for hurting someone.)

ACCEPT the consequences (by making right what you made wrong).

ALTER your behavior. (Change your attitudes and actions.)

ASK for forgiveness. (See Matt. 7:3–5; 1 John 1:8–9; Prov. 28:13.)

As the Seven A's indicate, removing these logs involves more than just confession; we must also change the way we think. Once we realize that our attitudes, words, and actions have been wrong, we must renounce our sin and turn to God. Depending on God to forgive us and change us—always remembering Jesus' wonderful work of salvation on the cross—will inspire and empower us to overcome the attitudes and habits that feed conflict.

This is difficult, but we have hope because God does not command us to do impossible things—he always offers the grace, power, and guidance necessary for us to do what he wants (2 Cor. 9:8).

Acknowledging our own contribution to a conflict will always bring us closer to our Lord and Savior and make us more useful instruments in his hands (1 John 1:9). And in many cases, it will lead to restored relationships and cooperation to find solutions that benefit everyone involved.

What would Mike and Peter do if they both decided to apply these biblical principles to their conflict?

Mike and Peter would each admit his sin and turn to God for forgiveness and help. In particular, Mike would ask God to help him be more discerning and sensitive about Peter's interests, and to grant him wisdom in dealing with his brother. And Peter would rely on God's grace to change his attitude toward his brother and to respond to him differently.

Mike would take responsibility for his contribution to the conflict, instead of looking for ways to escape from it by avoiding uncomfortable conversations. He would go to Peter and confess his failure to recognize how unevenly the estate was divided. If Mike were to take this step, it would likely soften Peter's heart and encourage him to be more open about his own responsibility in the conflict.

If Peter, by God's grace, looked closely at himself, he would see how angry, bitter, and self-righteous he had been toward his brother. He would admit this to Mike without excuses and would confess his tendency to use harsh words and criticism to manipulate and punish Mike.

Gently Restore

Having removed the logs from our own eyes, we can look at the next step in peacemaking: gently correcting and restoring our brother (Matt. 18:15). People have a wide range of responses to conflict. Some jump at the opportunity to get in an opponent's face and talk about something they are really interested in—*their opponent's* shortcomings. Other people entirely avoid correcting others, either because they fear it, or because they have bought into the world's pleasure-driven, "whatever you think is right for you" belief system that insists on letting people do their own thing, regardless of how sinful that "thing" is.

Neither of these responses is proper, nor is either biblical. The truth is, talking with others about their sin in a loving and helpful manner actually provides us an opportunity to serve them in a number of ways.

First, sometimes God can use us to help a person solve a problem more effectively than he could by himself. In fact, if we can learn to work together, our combined efforts can often result in a much better solution than either could have achieved alone.

Second, when we approach an individual in a loving and gracious way, God may use us to identify and lift a burden in his or her life. All too frequently, a conflict has less to do with stated issues and more to do with unresolved problems in the other's life. When people lash out, it is often a symptom of deeper problems. Instead of harshly confronting them—matching outburst for outburst or getting defensive—we can look for ways to help others lift the burdens that are beyond their ability to lift.

Third, God can use us to help others see their contributions to a conflict and recognize how they can change, in order to avoid similar problems in the future. This can lead to their repentance and a closer walk with the Lord. Both Jesus and Paul talk about the importance of approaching a brother caught in sin to help him see the error of his ways (Matt. 18:15; Gal. 6:1).

Finally, loving correction can serve as a positive example to others. Whether you realize it or not, people are constantly watching the way you handle adversity and treat those who wrong you. The way you act gives others a chance either to mock Christians and reject Christ or to become open to hearing the gospel. Furthermore, Christians watching your behavior will either feel it is all right to respond improperly to conflict or be encouraged to honor God in their own responses as well. Because imitation is a form of love, this last point is particularly true with children. Kids study the way their parents react to conflict and often imitate them when conflict arises in their own lives.

Before we approach someone about an offense, however, we should always consider overlooking the offense (Prov. 19:11). Many potential conflicts can be smothered before they ignite, simply by covering an offense with love and letting it go (1 Pet. 4:8). Generally, an offense is minor enough to be passed over if:

- it has not seriously dishonored God,
- it has not permanently damaged a relationship,
- it has not seriously hurt other people, and
- it is not seriously hurting the offender himself.

If an offense does not pass these guidelines, then it is too serious to overlook and should be dealt with.

When we engage people biblically, we will speak only to build them up. Words can be extremely powerful weapons, and the way we use them can make or break any attempt to resolve a conflict (Eph. 4:29).

If we are seeking restoration with someone, we will not give in to the tendency to lecture with a list of God's commands and the person's failures. Instead of condemning someone by dwelling primarily on his wrongs, we can bring hope by focusing mostly on what God has done through Jesus to forgive us and deliver us from our sins. For instance, if you need to talk to someone about his gossip, you might say,

> I don't think you deliberately set out to hurt Bill, but your words have hurt his reputation. The good news is that Jesus died to deliver you, me, and Bill—all of us—from our sins. God has given us both a warning and a wonderful promise: if we conceal our wrongs, he will continue to discipline us until we repent, but if we confess our sins, he will forgive us and restore us. There is such hope, because of what Jesus has done for us! If you ask for God's help and deal with this sin in the way his word teaches us to, the whole incident can be completely wiped away.

Good listening skills are also essential. Benefits include both understanding the problem on a practical level and communicating an attitude of humility, sincerity, genuine love, and concern to the other person.

Sometimes the first attempt to lovingly correct does not work; even repeated, thoughtful attempts at personal peacemaking may fail. In these cases it may become appropriate to ask friends, church leaders, or other neutral people to enter the discussion and assist in bringing about a resolution (Matt. 18:15).

What would it look like if Mike and Peter each approached the other to lovingly and graciously correct him?

Each brother would seek to encourage change in the other's life, gently helping him restore his relationship with God where it had been broken by sin. In addition, the men would work together with open and ongoing communication to prevent similar differences from happening in the future.

Mike would be willing to approach Peter as someone who recognizes the lifelong friendship he shared with his brother. He would intend both to listen to Peter's correction carefully, lovingly, and humbly, and to express tactfully his own concerns about Peter's sinful attitudes, words, and actions. Peter, on the other hand, would thoughtfully and graciously communicate to Mike how Mike had been insensitive to his financial interests and his stake in their father's business, especially in light of the many years they worked side by side under their father's leadership.

If each man confessed his own sins and sought to restore his brother, he would serve his family, the business employees, and their church in a significant way by setting a godly example of peacemaking. These genuine steps toward reconciliation would speak volumes to those watching from the "sidelines" about the two men's commitment to follow and honor Christ even in the midst of painful personal conflict.

Go and Be Reconciled

After we have gotten the logs out of our own eyes by confessing our contribution to a conflict, and after we have sought to serve our brother or sister by approaching him or her in love, it is time to seek reconciliation. Reconciliation is one of the most comforting words in the English language. Not only does the word stir our hearts—when we hear of a broken marriage restored, a church that embraces a repentant sinner, or long-estranged friends who resolve their differences—but it also expresses to us the spiritual reality of the dead being brought back to life.

Through the death of his Son, God has reconciled us to himself. He has shown his love for us in the most real and costly way possible, and he has made a way to bring his wandering children back to him to live in everlasting glory and joy. God has, in short, forgiven our many sins at an immeasurably great price.

And how do we, his children, react to such undeserved grace? We often have trouble forgiving others, even those we say we love. We qualify our forgiveness with such noncommittal statements as "I forgive you . . . I just don't want to be close to you again." Praise God that his forgiveness is not like that!

God makes it plain in his word that there is a direct connection between his forgiving us and our forgiving those who sin against us. The parable about the unmerciful servant (Matt. 18:23–35) and one request in the Lord's Prayer spell this out clearly: "Forgive us our debts as we have also forgiven our debtors" (Matt. 6:12; see also Col. 3:13).

Forgiveness is not a fuzzy, sentimental concept. Nor is it a feeling. Nor is it forgetting. God does not passively forget our sins; he actively chooses not to remember them (Jer. 31:34). Moreover, forgiveness is not excusing; the very fact that forgiveness is necessary indicates that someone did something wrong and inexcusable. And forgiveness is certainly not granting temporary pardon and storing up the memory of another's sin until we decide to use it later against him. Instead, forgiveness is an act of the will, an intentional decision to fully pardon our offender, to pay the debt he should have to pay.

But we cannot decide to forgive others in our own strength, especially when the hurt or betrayal is serious. There is only one way you can overcome the barriers to forgiveness: admit to God that you cannot forgive unless he changes your heart. This kind of honesty and reliance on God will open our hearts to his grace, and he will enable us to make the decision to forgive the other person and then carry it out.

When we forgive another person, we break down the wall that has risen between us and open the way for a renewed relationship. We set a person free from the penalty of being separated from us. This is a costly act on our part, because our human nature enjoys digging up past wrongs and flinging them back in the other person's face. But to truly forgive, we have to let the offending incident go.

To sum it up in more specific terms, forgiveness is a decision to make the following **Four Promises**:

- I will not dwell on this incident.
- I will not bring up this incident again and use it against you.
- I will not talk to others about this incident.

- I will not allow this incident to stand
  between us or hinder our personal
  relationship.

In effect, we are promising not to brood over the incident and not to allow the matter to keep a distance between us and anyone else. God models this kind of forgiveness—and we praise him for it. We can do no less than respond to others in the same way.

Regardless of how painful the offense is, by making these promises and delivering on them, we can with God's help imitate the forgiveness and reconciliation he offered us through the cross. By the grace of God, and only by his grace, can we forgive others as he has forgiven us.

What could reconciliation be like for Mike and Peter if they were faithful to God's promises?

Mike and Peter would welcome the opportunity to forgive each other, especially in light of God's great mercy toward them. Specifically, each brother would make an intentional decision to freely and fully pardon the other, so that their personal relationship and ongoing interactions would no longer be paralyzed by this conflict.

If both men were to look for the opportunities in this conflict to glorify God, serve each other, and grow in Christlikeness throughout the four-part process, they would develop helpful and creative ways to resolve their differences. They would also gain a deeper friendship and a growing trust in each other. Most importantly, they would have the peace and joy that comes from drawing near to God and experiencing his wonderful grace in their lives, even in the midst of conflict.

Making peace can be challenging and complicated. But God has graciously given us clear and helpful truths that are effective in any conflict. The four basic principles outlined in this booklet, the "Four G's," are drawn directly from the Bible. They provide a simple and highly effective framework for peacemaking that we have used for years in every imaginable conflict.

Perhaps there is a relationship in your life in which God is not being glorified, in which you and another person are not serving each other or growing to be more like Christ. If so, apply these principles from God's word. Thoughtfully read the Scriptures referred to in this booklet. Prayerfully begin to pursue peace in your relationship.

May the God who gives endurance and
encouragement give you
a spirit of unity among yourselves
as you follow Christ Jesus,
so that with one heart and mouth
you may glorify
the God and Father of our Lord
Jesus Christ. (Rom. 15:5–6)

GOD'S SEARCH AND RESCUE PLAN

Church Discipline

David V. Edling

No Way Out

Jake knew his life was in peril. What started as a great day of fun and adventure was now one of terror and loss. As he clung to the overturned hull of a chartered fishing vessel, his thoughts turned to how he would change his life if he could somehow escape the stormy waters that sought to engulf him. He was on the verge of drowning. The numbness in his feet and hands warned him that hypothermia must be setting in. How much time did he have? What chance of rescue?

Forty miles away, in the coastal city from which Jake had sailed with his friends earlier that day, Rich sat in his office with his head in his hands. "How had she ever found out?" That was the question plaguing his mind on the wet, cold afternoon. It started out innocent enough, but somehow his relationship with Beth, his attractive twenty-one-year-old secretary, had gotten out of control, and now his wife knew!

"What if the kids found out? Or any of the guys in my men's prayer group!"

To complicate matters, Rich knew he didn't want to give up the pleasures he was enjoying on his "golf Saturdays." And besides, Beth could potentially claim sexual harassment if he made her

mad. Then where would he be? No job, no future
... humiliated! Rich felt trapped. How much time
did he have? What chance of rescue?

A Desperate Situation

Jake . . .

How far out were they? Four hours of running at around ten or twelve knots . . . that would
mean at least forty or fifty miles. No land in sight.
No other boats. A Coast Guard helicopter could
be here in minutes if they just knew.

Had the operator sent out a call before the
vessel swamped and rolled? Jake hadn't seen the
ship's captain or any of his friends after being
tossed into the frigid water. He wondered if he
was alone. Had his friends already drowned or
were they over on the other side, clinging as he
was, or drifting away on pieces of wreckage?

In this cold, he couldn't hang on long. "Does
anybody know how desperate I am? Can anyone
help me?"

Rich . . .

"Hello, this is Rich." Rich swallowed hard
when he heard his pastor's voice on the other end

of the phone. He couldn't believe it! Linda had called their pastor asking what she should do if she knew a professing Christian was caught in sin. Now the pastor was calling to ask if he could meet with the two of them to discuss Linda's question!

What was going on? Pastor John hadn't said anything specific. How much had Linda told him? "Well, sure . . . ah . . . okay, Pastor John, tonight at 7:30 would be fine. We will be expecting you."

The Rescue Operation

Jake . . .

As Jake struggled to inch around the edge of the vessel, he caught a glimpse of something in the air. Soon a Coast Guard helicopter was hovering right over his head. Jake's heart pounded as he watched an orange-colored mesh basket dropping towards him. Everything was okay—he was being saved!

As the large basket lowered into the water next to him, Jake realized he would have to let go of the boat's hull and reach over to the floating basket. The ocean's swells kept everything moving, and his arms felt like lead. He was so cold and tired he could barely move. Were he to let go of the boat, he feared he would immediately sink straight down.

If only he had strapped on the life vest tucked behind his tackle box. He had never paid much attention to following rules or taking precautions. After all, he was young and strong. What would ever come his way that he couldn't handle? Now Jake's cockiness was something of the past. He felt helpless.

Rich . . .

Even if Linda hadn't told Pastor John anything specific, she must have said enough to prompt him to plan this face-to-face meeting. And certainly tonight it would all come out—all the details of his affair. Then everything would come tumbling down.

"What a mess! What can the pastor do to me? Probably something along the lines of that church discipline stuff! I'll be kicked out of the church and publicly humiliated. Linda will probably want a divorce, and I'll hardly ever see the kids again." Rich felt like he was on the verge of drowning. He felt helpless.

Saved by the Sacrifice of Another

Jake . . .

Lifting his head skyward, Jake wanted to yell that he couldn't do it. He couldn't grab the basket and pull himself to safety. There was no way he could save himself. Then he saw a man jumping out of the helicopter! "I can't rescue myself," Jake thought, "so some Coast Guardsman is risking his life for mine."

With powerful, confident strokes, Petty Officer Doug James swam to Jake and relayed the plan to get him on board the hovering helicopter. Within minutes Jake was flying above the waves, wrapped in a warm blanket, and receiving first-rate care from several Coast Guardsmen. He was the only survivor.

Rich . . .

That evening, Pastor John sat across from Rich and Linda in their living room. He shared that he had come because he sensed from his conversation with Linda that something serious was going on. After beginning with a short prayer, he opened his Bible and read from Ezekiel 34 in order to explain his responsibility to faithfully shepherd them. "I will search for the lost and bring back the strays. I will bind up the injured and strengthen the weak. . . . "

Rich was hearing, but his mind was in a fog. "What did this passage have to do with Linda's question? Or with him?"

Pastor John explained, "Linda, the question you asked about a believer caught in sin is at the very heart of the whole message of the Bible. When someone has placed his trust in Christ and has professed that faith publicly in joining the church, he has become part of God's flock, of God's family. A special relationship has formed—a bond—and the church is called on in a very special way to be there whenever one of its members finds himself in danger, especially when sin has taken him captive."

Pastor John flipped in his Bible to chapter 18 of Matthew and asked Rich if he would begin reading at verse one. Rich read, "At that time the disciples came to Jesus and asked, 'Who is the greatest in the kingdom of heaven?'"

The pastor stopped Rich. He explained that the whole rest of the chapter is a response to that question. Rich remembered that the disciples seemed to have a recurring interest in which one of them would be the greatest, even arguing about it during the Last Supper!

Pastor John went on to explain how people often misunderstand Jesus' teaching here because they don't understand that the disciples' question provides the context for the rest of the passage. Jesus is answering a specific question, which, at its heart, deals with the theme of relationships within the kingdom.

Rich read the next several verses. The pastor noted how gentle Jesus was in his teaching by using the example of a little child he beckoned to join them. This child, Jesus says, has believed in him for eternal life. The passage then goes on to talk about the great sinfulness of sin (vv. 6–9) and how Christians have a special relationship to God, even when they are tempted by sin (v. 10).

Rich was waiting for the pastor to get to the bottom line in order to open the door for Linda to tell him all about Rich's sin. He started thinking of excuses for his behavior. Pastor John then asked Linda if she would read verses 12–14, the parable of the lost sheep.

"What do you think?" Linda began reading. "If a man owns a hundred sheep, and one of them wanders away, will he not leave the ninety-nine on the hills and go to look for the one that wandered off? And if he finds it, I tell you the truth, he is happier about that one sheep than about the ninety-nine that did not wander off. In the same way, your Father in heaven is not willing that any of these little ones should be lost."

Rich again was perplexed. What does a story about evangelism have to do with this situation? As if reading his mind, Pastor John said, "You have probably heard sermons or read things about this parable that assume it is talking about evangelism. Because it uses the word "lost," most people think it is talking about seeking and saving those who have not placed their trust in Jesus for eternal life. But in context, it cannot mean that for several reasons.

"First, in response to the question posed in verse one, remember that Jesus is talking about the relationships of those who are saved and within the kingdom. Second, notice that he carries the example he used earlier of a 'little child' into this parable, and Jesus refers to "these little ones" as people who believe in him.

"Third, the word 'sheep' is used throughout Scripture as referring to those who are a part of the family, his family. In other words, they are those who have believed. For example, in John 10:14–16, Jesus says, 'I am the good shepherd; I know my sheep and my sheep know me—just as the Father knows me and I know my Father— and I lay down my life for the sheep!' Also, in verses 27–30 of that same chapter, he proclaims, 'My sheep listen to my voice; I know them, and they follow me. I give them eternal life, and they shall never perish; no one can snatch them out of my hand. My Father who has given them to me, is greater than all; no one can snatch them out of my Father's hand. I and the Father are one.'"

Pastor John continued, "If we understand that this parable is directed toward believers who need rescuing from sin, it should be a great comfort to us. Jesus uses it to convince us that when a beloved believer, one of his flock, falls into sin, extraordinary efforts should be made to bring him back into fellowship. That action, Linda, goes directly to the point of your question."

Linda nodded, but then shared, "While I see God's motive for seeking to restore one of his children from sin, I don't understand how that can be accomplished."

John responded, "That's what we come to next—the means and methods that Christians are to use to make the rescue! The process described in Matthew 18:15–20—what we call 'church discipline'—is actually God's search and rescue plan for seeking to restore a brother or sister lost in his or her sin.

"These steps guide us in responding appropriately to someone based on the nature of his sin and his spiritual readiness to respond. According to verse 15, the person most affected by the sin should initiate a personal, private discussion with this individual. The process slowly progresses to include others, if, and only if, the person being confronted is unwilling to listen, turn, and repent."

Rich jumped in, "You mean, if someone immediately repents and confesses to that one person, no one else needs to be involved or even hear about the situation?"

"In most circumstances," John replied, "that's right. The matter is finished and over with if his confession is genuine, and if he stops sinning, does all he can to change, and makes whatever restitution is necessary to the one he's wronged. If he has sinned against others, he needs to demonstrate his repentance and confess his sins to them as well.

"Only in the case that he refuses to listen—that is, if he fails to acknowledge his sin and his need to repent, confess, and receive forgiveness—would the person who was wronged proceed to the next steps. I'll never forget what one of my seminary professors said about the purpose of church discipline. He said, 'Discipline is not just an exercise of negative judgment, a matter of church courts and censures. It begins with the care of friends with whom we strive to follow Christ, and to whom we are, in a measure, accountable.'[2] It's only when sin continues that the full weight and authority

2. Edmond P. Clowney, *The Church* (Downers Grove, IL: InterVarsity Press, 1995).

of Christ, acting through the church, comes into play. And that can be a powerful force to turn a Christian away from his sin.

"Rich, are you familiar with the story in 1 Corinthians chapter 5 of the man caught in sexual sin?" Rich mumbled that he was.

Pastor John continued, "The thing I like best about chapter 18 of Matthew is what comes right after Jesus has taught the steps of the search and rescue plan. Peter, old lovable Peter, after hearing all this, asks Jesus, 'Lord, how many times shall I forgive my brother when he sins against me? Up to seven times?' This uneducated fisherman gets it! He realizes that what Jesus has been talking about is forgiveness, a rescue plan that leads to restoration and reconciliation. Where sin has built barriers, forgiveness tears them down!

"Then Jesus tells one of the most powerful parables recorded in Scripture, the parable of the unmerciful servant. God's forgiveness is unimaginably expansive! And because he has forgiven each of us so much, how much more should we be ready and willing to forgive those who have sinned against us?"

"It all fits," Linda said. "It's almost as if those two parables that express God's great love for his sheep serve as bookends to support the 'book' you're talking about—God's search and rescue plan found in verses 15–20!"

"Yes! And it's amazing to me," remarked Pastor John, "how everybody loves those bookends, but turns up his nose at God's greatest expression of care—the book supported between them! Can you imagine how crazy it would be for a Coast Guard helicopter rescue team to fly out, hover over a sinking vessel with injured and near-death sailors, and merely yell to them, pointing in the direction of the land so they could begin swimming?

"No! Of course not! What does that helicopter crew do? They lower a rescue basket, and if the survivors are about to slip away and can't climb into that basket, the pilot commands one of his crewmen to jump out and risk his own life to save those who are about to perish. In Ezekiel 34, that is exactly what the shepherds of Israel failed to do—jump out and seek the lost and bind up the wounds of the injured."

Just then the phone rang. Rich walked into the kitchen to answer it. "Rich, it's Jake. You're not going to believe what happened to me today. I would have drowned if I hadn't been rescued!"

Rich responded, "Jake, I can believe it because I think I am about to be rescued myself."

Friend, do you feel like you are playing the game of the hypocrite, professing to faith in Christ, yet swimming in the stormy waters of unrepentant sin? The church is there to rescue you. The biblical process of loving confrontation and the involvement of others to help you come to your senses is God's plan for eternal good in your life, now and forever. Seek out a church that lovingly practices church discipline, submit to their authority by becoming a member, and reap the rewards God intends for you. If you are already a member of a church but don't know if it practices church discipline, go to your church leaders and ask them. Share with them what you have learned in this little book. If they need help establishing the practices and policies of church discipline, have them contact us at Peacemaker Ministries (www.peacemaker.net).

Additional Resources

For further insight into the biblical principles, purposes, and practice of church discipline, the following resources are recommended:

Handbook of Church Discipline by Jay E. Adams, Grand Rapids: Zondervan, 1986.

The Peacemaker—A Biblical Guide to Resolving Personal Conflict by Ken Sande, Grand Rapids: Baker Books, 1997.

That We May Share His Holiness—A Fresh Approach to Church Discipline by James T. (Tommy) South, Abilene: Bible Guides, 1997.

This book in Peacemaker Ministries' Culture of Peace Series is dedicated to the brave men and women of the United States Coast Guard who place their lives at risk to save others. It is also dedicated to those faithful pastors who fearlessly speak the truth in love to rescue those who face a far greater eternal peril when sin isn't taken seriously. Our churches should be filled with stories of rescues, just as are the annals of the U.S. Coast Guard.

Words That Cut

Learning to Take Criticism in Light of the Gospel

Rev. Alfred Poirier

Words can cut to the core. Undoubtedly, you know that from experience. At times they hurt so much that we turn away and refuse to listen. Sadly, the refusal to hear such words can lead to real and great tragedy.

On January 28, 1986, the space shuttle *Challenger* and its crew embarked on a mission to broaden educational horizons and promote the advancement of scientific knowledge. The most outstanding objective of the *Challenger* 51-L mission was for crew member and teacher Christa McAuliffe to present educational lessons from space. The mission did present a lesson, but not one that anyone expected.

Just seventy-five seconds after lift off, tragedy struck. Before a watching world the shuttle suddenly erupted overhead—disintegrating the cabin along with its crew. The debris of metal, blood, and bones plummeted to earth, and along with it, our nation's glory.

What had gone wrong? That was the pressing question everyone was asking. As teams of researchers examined the wreckage, the specific cause was soon discovered. The problem was with the O-rings (circular rubber seals), which had been designed to fit snugly into the joints of the booster engine sections.

Evidently, the O-rings had become defective under adverse conditions, and the resulting mechanical failure led to the tragedy. That was the whole story. Or so many thought. But then the truth came out.

The *New York Times* put it frankly: the ultimate cause of the space shuttle disaster was *pride*. A group of top-level managers failed to listen carefully to the warnings, advice, and criticism given by those beneath them in the chain of command. Those in lower management were concerned about the operational reliability of certain parts of the booster engine when under conditions of abnormal stress. They expressed their concerns about the O-rings, but the upper management did not listen. Just think: *heeding a little criticism could have saved seven human lives.*

The tragedy of the *Challenger* presents a challenge relevant to all of us: Do we know how to take criticism? How should we respond to words that "cut to the core"? Criticism is constantly zigzagging its way in and out of our lives. In fact, how we take criticism plays a major role in how we respond to the conflicted situations we deal with daily: Will we respond with a spirit of defensiveness and pride, heightening the conflict? Or will we respond with wisdom, graciousness, and humility, thereby reducing the level of hostility?

The answer to these questions has already been given. God has given us his gift of the cross. Through understanding and embracing the gospel of Jesus Christ's death on the cross, we have the very thing needed to help us respond to criticism in a way that pleases God.

Our Natural Response to Criticism

"Criticism" is *when another person judges you by declaring that you have fallen short of a particular standard.* The standard may be God's or man's. The judgment may be true or false. The criticism may be given gently to correct, or harshly to condemn. It may come from a friend or an enemy. Whatever the case, it is a judgment about you—that you have failed and fallen short of someone's standard.

However criticism comes, most of us would agree that it is simply difficult to take. Criticism stings! And who of us doesn't know someone with whom we need to be especially careful, lest even our most subtle suggestions for improvement spark his anger? How many times have you been warned to "walk on eggshells" around *that* person?

Unfortunately, the case is too often true that "that person" is someone in a position of authority or leadership—such as a parent, a husband, a church leader, or an employer. Those under his authority would not dare confront or criticize him for fear that he might lash out in anger or even retaliate. How many women hesitate to criticize their husband for fear that he might bristle or walk off without listening? How many church members have chosen not to confront their pastor for fear that he will condemn their remarks as accusatory and unloving? The consequences in these types of situations range from estranged marriages to people walking out on their church or ministry.

What is even worse is that many people in positions of authority either surround themselves with "yes" people—who never say "no" or question their decisions—or "condition" those who live and work with them to be agreeable . . . or else!!! How many children are taught that you *never* question Mom or Dad, not even with a respectful appeal? How many employees fear they're limiting their chances for promotion if they suggest a different way of doing something?

As sad as this is, such people differ little from me. I, too, do not like criticism and find it very hard to take. I'd much rather be commended than corrected, praised than rebuked. I'd much rather judge than be judged! And I am not alone in this. The more I listen, the more I hear people pulling out their swords to put up a defense when confronted with criticism.

Perhaps you've seen it in marriage in the humorous way a couple is sidetracked from the issue at hand into endless bickering about who said what, when, and where. Or what about the mother and daughter who go back and forth correcting one another about whether it was a Tuesday or Wednesday when something happened?

Why do we spend so much time and energy swatting at these flies with sledgehammers? When someone points out our most minor shortcomings, why does it provoke us to a full-scale attack? Why do our hearts and minds so instantly engage, and our emotions surge with energy, running to our defense?

The answer is simple. These issues are *not* minor or insignificant. We defend what we believe to be of great value. We believe something much larger will be lost if we do not use every means to rescue it—specifically, *our* name, *our* reputation, *our* honor, and *our* glory. Indeed, we think it is *our* life that we are saving.

In effect, we say to ourselves, "If *I* don't point out that *I've* been misunderstood, misquoted, and falsely accused, then others won't know that *I'm right*. And if *I* don't point out *my* rightness, nobody will. *I* will be scorned and condemned in the eyes of others, and *I* can't live with that."

Do you recognize the *idol of self* here—
the deep-rooted desire to place ourselves, our
reputation, and our honor above all else? Do you
see the controlling desire for self-justification—
to be proven right (or righteous) in the eyes of
others? Unfortunately, our idols have consequences. This deep desire to justify ourselves
results in the tragedy of the space shuttle getting played out over and over again in our lives.
It destroys our relationships. It leads to death.
For the sake of our pride and foolishness, we
willingly suffer the loss of friends, a spouse, or
loved ones.

Some of this destruction comes veiled as a
truce. We call for a cold war; we make a false
peace. We pledge to each other to discuss only
those things that have little significance for bet-
tering our souls. We speak at the most superfi-
cial level. In the meantime, we bury land mines
to threaten the other, letting him know that we
will explode if he so much as peeps a word about
my mistake, *my* error, *my* sin, or *my* need to be
corrected.

In short, our idolatrous desire to justify ourselves fuels our inability to take criticism, which,
in turn, is the cause for much conflict. It is the
reason that many marriages and families split,
factions form, and relationships grow cold. And
it is the reason we so desperately need the di-

rection provided in Scripture to begin forming a redemptive, godward view of criticism.

The Biblical Response to Criticism

Scripture, particularly the book of Proverbs, teaches how important it is to be able to hear correction and take criticism. According to the following verses, being teachable and willing to receive correction is a mark of the mature:

- The way of a fool seems right to him, but a wise man *listens to advice* (Prov. 12:15).
- Pride only breeds quarrels, but wisdom is found in those who *take advice* (Prov. 13:10).
- A rebuke *impresses* a man of discernment more than a hundred lashes a fool (Prov. 17:10; italics added in each verse).

Moreover, the wise father and mother will encourage, as well as model, such a spirit of wisdom and willingness to their children.

The ability to take advice, correction, and rebuke is not only considered a *mark* of the wise—and the inability to do so, a mark of the fool—but it is also thought to determine the *path* of the wise. In fact, Scripture tells us that both the wise and the foolish *reap consequences* according to their ability to take criticism:

- He who scorns instruction *will pay for it*, but he who respects a command is *rewarded* (Prov. 13:13).
- Instruct a wise man and he *will be wiser still*; teach a righteous man and he *will add to his learning* (Prov. 9:9).
- He who ignores discipline despises himself, but whoever heeds correction *gains understanding* (Prov. 15:32; italics added in each verse).

The wise recognize that there is gain in taking criticism. No wonder David exclaims in Psalm 141:5, "Let a righteous man strike me—it is a *kindness*; let him rebuke me—it is *oil on my head*. My head *will not refuse it*" (italics added). David knows the benefit of gaining wisdom, knowledge, and understanding. And he knows criticism is a kindness, a blessing, and an honor, *even if misdirected or delivered destructively*.

Is that how you look at a rebuke? Is this how you hear criticism, correction, or counsel? Do you *want* to change the way you respond to criticism? That is a key question. We must want it. But wanting is not having. How can we move from being quick to defend ourselves against any and all criticism, toward becoming like David who welcomed it as a kindness?

The answer lies in understanding, believing, and affirming all that God says about us in the cross of Christ. We need to embrace the apostle Paul's claim that we "have been crucified with Christ" (Gal. 2:20) by condemning all that God condemns and affirming all that God affirms in Christ's crucifixion. In other words, we will never be able to welcome criticism as a kindness until we understand both God's *criticism* and his *justification* of us through Christ's cross.

The Criticism of the Cross

The first step in understanding and applying the cross is to be able to say, "In Christ's cross, I affirm God's *judgment* of me." As we've seen, criticism is another word for "judgment." One reason we find it hard to hear criticism from others is because we have not heard God's criticism of us on the cross. We forget that on the cross God "criticized" us—that is, God judged us *in Christ.* That is why Paul the apostle declares, "I have been crucified with Christ" (Gal. 2:20).

Have you ever claimed, "I have been crucified with Christ" and believed it for yourself? Part of what this entails is recognizing and agreeing with God's judgment of each of us—that I have *sinned against him*. There is no escaping the truth: "There is no one righteous, not even one" (Rom. 3:9–18). In response to my sin, the cross has criticized and judged me more intensely, deeply, pervasively, and truly than anyone else ever could; no one else's criticism of me could match the thoroughness of God's criticism of me.

Knowing this permits us to respond to all other criticism leveled at us by saying, "That is just a fraction of it." Doesn't Scripture teach us this?

- "Cursed is everyone who does not continue to do everything written in the Book of the Law" (Gal. 3:10).
- "For whoever keeps the whole law and yet stumbles at just one point is guilty of breaking all of it" (James 2:10).

In other words, we can strongly agree with the criticism made of us because Scripture has already condemned us for failing to keep the whole law, and for breaking the entire law. In light of these massive charges against us, any accusations launched at us are mere understatements about who we are and what we've done!

The cross not only criticizes me as a sinner, but it also condemns me as a lawbreaker. The person who says, "I have been crucified with Christ" is a person well aware of his inability to keep the law. You'll never get life right by your own unaided efforts because, as Galatians 3:10 once again tells us, all who rely on keeping the law are under a curse: "Cursed is *everyone* who does not continue to do *everything* written in the Book of the Law" (italics added).

Furthermore, we cannot defend ourselves as lawbreakers by trying to offset our sin with our good works. Look again at James 2:10 and consider this fact: "Whoever keeps the whole law and yet stumbles at just one point is guilty of breaking all of it." Good works cannot make up for that! Once again we see that the cross does not merely criticize or judge us as sinners; it condemns us for not doing *everything* written in God's law.

Do you believe that? Do you feel the force of that criticism? Do you appreciate the thoroughness of God's judgment?

Finally, in light of the cross, I believe that my sin and my inability to keep the law deserve the ultimate judgment—death. Paul warns in Romans 6:23, "The wages of sin is death." As believers in Christ, we claim this truth when we say along with Paul, "I have been crucified with Christ and *I no longer live*" (Gal. 2:20; italics added), and "*Our old self was crucified with him* so that the body of sin might be done away with" (Rom. 6:6; italics added). In other words, our sin deserves death, and in the cross, our sin has been put to death.

Do you feel the force of that criticism? Do you appreciate the thoroughness of God's judgment?

To claim to be a Christian is to claim to be a person who has understood criticism. The Christian is a person who has *stood under* the greatest criticism—*God's* criticism—and agreed with it! As people who have been "crucified with Christ," we acknowledge, agree, and approve of God's judgments against us. We confess, "I am a sinner! I am a lawbreaker! I deserve death!" Do you see how radical a confession that is?

But we can say more: We can proclaim and rejoice in the glorious reality of our justification in Christ.

The Justification of the Cross

Second, in order to understand and apply the cross, we must be able to claim, "In Christ's cross, I affirm God's *justification* of me." To respond to criticism wisely, I must not only agree with God's judgment of me in the cross of Christ, but I must also agree with God's justification of me—a sinner.

On the basis of Christ's sacrificial death on the cross, God justifies ungodly people. Let's think about this for a moment. First, notice that he *justifies* ungodly people. In other words, Christ has paid the penalty of our sin, and God has reckoned Christ's righteousness as our own (Phil. 3:9) by faith in him.

So we are justified—or declared "righteous"—in God's sight. What a glorious truth!

Second, notice that God justifies *ungodly people* (Rom. 3:20–26; 4:5). In other words, he justifies those who know their sin and trust *only* in God for their salvation—not in their own effort or good works.

This is what makes us boast not in ourselves, but in Christ. When I hear criticism with ears of unbelief, I defend myself by boasting about my works and my performance. But that is not the way of true faith. Faith in Christ hears and answers criticism by saying, "The life I live in the body, I live by faith in the Son of God, who loved me and gave himself for me" (Gal. 2:20). No longer do I try to protect and boast about my righteousness. Now I boast in Christ's righteousness. It is his righteousness that I receive by faith, not by my performance.

Solomon says pride breeds quarrels. Quarrels are often over who is right; they are the result of our idolatrous demand for self-justification.

But they can be silenced in the cross. For it is there that *God* justifies me—that *he* declares me righteous—by grace alone and through faith alone in Christ alone. And it is there that I am reminded that the Son of God loved me and gave himself for me. Because of this, God has thoroughly accepted me in Christ.

What a sure foundation for the soul! Now, I don't practice self-justification, but boasting—boasting about Christ's righteousness for me and his acceptance of me.

If you truly take this to heart, the whole world can stand against you, denounce you, or criticize you, and you can reply, "If God has justified me, who can condemn me? If God declares me righteous, accepts me, and will never forsake me, then why should I feel insecure and fear criticism? Christ bore my sins, and I received his righteousness. Christ takes my condemnation, and I receive God's great approval—'Justified!'" And you can begin to carry out the implications of these great truths in your life.

Implications for Responding to Criticism

In light of both God's judgment and justification of the sinner in the cross of Christ, we can begin to discover how to deal with any and all criticism.

First, we can face any criticism that someone may cast against us. In other words, no criticism from another can be greater than the cross's criticism of me—a criticism to which I've already agreed. If I know myself as crucified with Christ, I can receive criticism with this attitude: "You do not know a fraction of my shortcomings. Christ has said more about my sin, my failings, my rebellion, and my foolishness than any man can say about me."

The implications of this reality should play a major role in shaping how we respond to criticism:

- We can respond with a *spirit of thanksgiving.* Rather than perceiving the most devastating criticism as a strike against who we are and everything we stand for, we can begin to see it as a sweet mercy. Like David we will be able to declare, "Let a righteous man strike me—it is a kindness" (Ps. 141:5). As we consider the accusation brought against us, we will be able to think, "I am thankful for this correction. It is a blessing to me. For even if it is wrong or misplaced, it reminds me of my true faults and sins for which my Lord and Savior paid dearly when he died on the cross for me."

- We can respond with the *humility and willingness to hear all criticism*. If we truly believe that criticism is a mercy and a kindness, we will be willing to hear it constructively—with the patience to discern and distinguish what is truly valid. Knowing both God's judgment and justification of us in the cross, we will not be surprised to hear of our blind spots or hidden faults. God has judged all our sins; Christ has covered all our sins. So we can listen to those criticizing us and say, "I want to learn how your criticisms are valid. Help me to understand them."

- We can respond with a *spirit of surrender*. No longer do we have to battle the condemnation of criticism, because God has justified us. As the apostle Paul declares, "Who will bring any charge against those whom God has chosen? It is God who justifies. Who is he that condemns?" (Rom. 8:33–34). So we can accept criticism graciously, rather than reacting with bitterness, defensiveness, or blame-shifting—responses that typically

worsen and intensify conflict and lead to
the breakdown of relationships.

Not surprisingly, such gospel-permeated
responses to criticism often help minimize the
anger and frustration of those who are launch-
ing the criticism. When they see that you do
not desire to minimize your wrongs and shift
the blame—but to take their counsel seriously—
they tend to qualify their criticism. Instead of
charging "You never . . . ," they suggest "Sometimes you . . ." Rather than diving further into
conflict, they willingly give you a little grace.

*Second, we can see God's hand in criticism and
seek to respond wisely.* We must remember that
all the corrections and advice we receive from
others (even those that are unfair and mean-spir-
ited) are sent from our heavenly Father—through
his good, wise, and perfect providence. They are
his corrections, *his* rebukes, *his* warnings, *his*
scoldings. David knows this when Shimei cruelly
curses him (see 2 Sam. 16:5–7). David's men want
to kill Shimei, but David commands, "Leave him
alone; let him curse, *for the LORD has told him
to*. It may be that the LORD will see my distress
and repay me with good for the cursing I am
receiving today" (2 Sam. 16:11–12; italics added).
David sees that those who criticize him are ultimately sent by God. Instead of defending himself

or attacking his accusers, he submits himself to the Lord.

Likewise, when we hear criticism, we should try to respond in a spirit of submission, recognizing that it is God's means of humbling us and weeding out the pride in our hearts. But he doesn't stop there—his purposes are much greater. He is seeking to *replace* our pride with understanding, goodness, and truth. He is teaching us to discern how to respond *wisely* to criticism—however just or unjust it may be. For example, someone who has heard harsh and unfair criticism knows from experience how hurtful these words can be. One way he can respond wisely is by learning how to give criticism graciously and constructively.

The implications of taking criticism in light of the Cross are far-reaching. We do not have to fear man's criticism, for we have already agreed with God's criticism. And we do not have to seek man's approval, for we have something much better—God's approval. His love for us helps us to hear correction and criticism as kindness from our Father, who loves each of us and says, "My son, do not make light of the Lord's discipline, and do not lose heart when he rebukes you, because the Lord disciplines those he loves, and he punishes everyone he accepts as a son" (Heb. 12:5–6).

Applying What We've Learned

Perhaps you are convicted about how you take criticism, and desire to grow in this area. Perhaps you understand both the criticism and the justification of the cross, and how each shapes your response to criticism. But there is still a disconnect: "How," you ask, "do I 'plug in' my desire to change and my understanding of the cross in order to feel the current of true change flowing through my life?" In other words, how do you apply what you've learned in order to see real results in your life? Following is a list of practical steps to begin that process:

Critique yourself. How do I typically react to correction? Do I pout? Do I try to play down my error and shift the blame? Do I seek to defend myself, boasting about my "good deeds" in order to prove that I am better than another? Or do I go on the attack and point out the other person's sin or error?

And how often do I take advice? How often do I seek it? Are people able to approach me to correct me? Can my spouse, parents, children, siblings, or friends correct me? Am I a teachable person? Do I harbor anger against the person who criticizes me?

Ask the Lord to give you the desire to be wise instead of foolish. Use Proverbs to remind yourself how good it is to be willing to receive criticism, advice, rebuke, counsel, or correction. Meditate upon the following passages: Proverbs 9:9; 12:15; 13:10, 13; 15:32; 17:10; and Psalm 141:5.

Focus on your crucifixion with Christ. While you might say, "I have been crucified with Christ," you may not find yourself walking daily in the light of the cross. Give thanks to God for his justification of you. Then challenge yourself with these two questions:

1. If I continually kick under the criticism of others, how can I say I know and agree with the criticism of the cross?

2. If I typically justify myself, how can I say I know, love, and cling to God's justification of me through Christ?

This process will drive you back to the cross to reflect on God's judgment and justification of you, a sinful sinner. As you meditate on what God has done for you, you will find your faith directed to Christ. And it is by faith that you will again affirm all that God says about you in Christ, with whom you have been crucified.

Learn to speak nourishing words to others. I want to receive criticism as a sinner living within Jesus' mercy. So how can I give criticism in a way that expresses mercy to another? Accurate, balanced criticism given mercifully is the easiest to hear. And if I recognize that my sinful pride rebels against even that kind of criticism, I will strive to speak the truth in love to others. I will work to be kind to everyone, not resentful, teaching gently (see 2 Tim. 2:24–26). And I will ask, "How can I best give accurate, fair, and balanced criticism with much mercy and affirmation?"

My prayer is that as you struggle against the sin of self-justification and learn to take criticism, you will deepen your love for the glory of God as revealed in the gospel of his Son, and you will grow wise by faith.

Judging Others

The Danger of Playing God

By Ken Sande

I Knew It!

I knew he was too proud to take criticism," thought Anne, "and now I have proof!"

On the previous Sunday, Anne had dropped a prayer card in the offering plate asking her pastor to stop in and pray with her when she went to the hospital for some minor surgery. When he failed to come by, she called the church secretary and learned that her pastor had already been to the hospital that day to see another church member.

"So he has no excuse!" she thought. "He was in the building and knew I needed his support, but still he ignored me. He's resented me ever since I told him his sermons lack practical application. Now he's getting back at me by ignoring my spiritual needs. And he calls himself a shepherd!"

After brooding over his rejection for three days, Anne sat down Saturday evening and wrote a letter confronting her pastor about his pride, defensiveness, and hypocrisy. As she sealed the envelope, she could not help thinking about the conviction he would feel when he opened his mail.

The moment she walked into church the next morning, one of the deacons hurried over to her. "Anne, I need to apologize to you. When I took the prayer cards out of the offering plates last week, I accidentally left your card with some pledge cards. I didn't notice my mistake until last night when I was totaling the pledges. I am so sorry I didn't get your request to the pastor!" Before Anne could reply to the deacon, her pastor approached her with a warm smile. "Anne, I was thinking about your comment about practical application as I finished my sermon yesterday. I hope you notice the difference in today's message."

Anne was speechless. All she could think about was the letter she had just dropped in a mailbox three blocks from church.

Judging Is Necessary but Dangerous

As Anne discovered, judging others can put us in embarrassing situations. Does this mean that we should never judge others? Not at all. As you interact with other people you must constantly interpret, evaluate, and form opinions regarding their qualities, words, and actions, so that you may respond to them appropriately (see Prov. 8:12–21; 9:1–6; Matt. 10:16; 1 Cor. 2:11–16).

For example, when you buy something, you need to decide whether the seller is being honest about its quality and value. If someone disregards your advice, you need to interpret her actions so you can approach her more effectively. And when someone is nominated to a church of-

fice, the congregation needs to evaluate whether
he is qualified to serve.

Although judging is a normal and necessary
part of life, Scripture warns us that we have a
natural tendency to judge others in a wrong way.
For example, Jesus says:

> "Do not judge, or you too will be judged. For
> in the same way you judge others, you will be
> judged, and with the measure you use, it will be
> measured to you. Why do you look at the speck
> of sawdust in your brother's eye and pay no
> attention to the plank in your own eye? How
> can you say to your brother, 'Let me take the
> speck out of your eye,' when all the time there
> is a plank in your own eye? You hypocrite, first
> take the plank out of your own eye, and then
> you will see clearly to remove the speck from
> your brother's eye." (Matt. 7:1–6)

As this passage teaches, when we evaluate
and judge other people, our natural inclination
is to ignore our own faults and to make critical
judgments of others. Jesus is not forbidding *critical thinking* in the positive sense, which is eval-
uating others' words and actions carefully so we
can discriminate between truth and error, right
and wrong (see Matt. 7:15–16).

What he is warning us about is our inclination to make *critical judgments* in the negative

sense, which involves looking for others' faults
and, without valid and sufficient reason, forming unfavorable opinions of their qualities, words,
actions, or motives. In simple terms, it means
looking for the worst in others.

Critical Judgments Come Naturally

When Adam sinned, he corrupted the entire
human race. He passed on to each of us an inher-
ent tendency to sin, which includes a natural inclination towards mistaken, negative judgments.[1]
This inclination is revealed throughout the Bible.
The Old Testament offers many examples:

- After the Israelites conquered the prom-
  ised land, the tribes of Reuben, Gad, and
  the half tribe of Manasseh returned to
  their allotted land and built an altar by
  the Jordan. When the other tribes heard
  about the altar, they assumed the worst
  and rashly assembled their troops to
  go to war against their brothers. Fortu-
  nately, before a battle began, those who

---

1. In fact, we also have a tendency to make mistaken, positive assessments! We can be impressed by
things we ought to criticize (2 Tim. 4:3; 2 Cor. 11:4;
Gal. 1:6–9; 1 Sam. 16:6f.; Prov. 7, etc.).

had built the altar were able to explain
its legitimate purpose and avoid blood-
shed (Josh. 22:10–34).

- In 1 Samuel, we read how the high
  priest made a hasty, critical judgment.
  When Eli saw Hannah praying in the
  temple, moving her lips but making no
  sound, he concluded that she was drunk.
  Only after harshly confronting her
  did he learn that she was communing
  with the Lord in a way that put Eli
  to shame (1:12–17).

- Even King David made critical judgments. When he fled from his son
  Absalom, a man named Ziba brought
  David a critical report regarding Saul's
  son, Mephibosheth, saying that he had
  turned against King David. Without
  waiting to hear Mephibosheth's side
  of the story, David passed judgment
  against this innocent man and turned
  all of his property over to a false witness (2 Sam. 16:1–4; 19:24–30).

The New Testament also portrays this pattern of making critical judgments.

- When Jesus was doing miracles and healing the blind, the Pharisees stubbornly

closed their eyes to the good he was doing and interpreted his actions in the worst possible way, saying that he was actually serving the devil (Matt. 12:22–24).

- In Acts 21:26–29, we see that Paul meticulously followed all of the Jewish customs as he prepared to come into the temple. Even so, the Jews assumed the worst, jumping to the conclusion that he had defiled the temple and should be stoned.

- As 1 Corinthians 10–11 reveals, the Apostle Paul repeatedly was condemned falsely, not only by the Jews, but also by people from within the Christian community. Like many church leaders today, he learned the hard lesson that servants of the Lord are often misunderstood, criticized, and judged by the very people they are trying to serve.

But we don't need to look back thousands of years to see people making critical judgments of others. Just think how easily we ourselves believe the worst about others' motives or actions.

- If someone delays answering a letter or fulfilling a commitment, we too easily assume he is avoiding us or evading his responsibilities. Could it be that he's been in the hospital recovering from a serious accident? Could he be overwhelmed by other responsibilities?

- If our children do not complete their chores on time, we conclude that they are being disobedient. Could it be that they are secretly wrapping a special present for their mom's birthday? Could they have gotten distracted, and a simple reminder would help?

- If an employer fails to give us a raise, we assume she is unappreciative or greedy. Could she be struggling to keep the business going in the face of increasing competition and operating costs?

- If someone at church seems unfriendly, we assume she is proud or aloof. Could it be that she feels awkward and unsure of herself and is hoping someone will reach out to her?

- If the elders do not accept a proposal we make, we may conclude that they are narrow-minded and do not understand or appreciate our opinions or needs. Could it be that God is leading them to give priority to a different ministry?

- If church members raise questions about policies or new programs, church leaders may conclude that the members are stubbornly unwilling to consider new ideas or stretch themselves to grow. They may even be labeled as rebellious troublemakers. Could it be that they have legitimate insights and concerns that deserve a careful hearing?

Judge Charitably

Instead of judging others *critically*, God commands us to judge charitably. The church has historically used the word "charitable" as a synonym for the word "loving." This has resulted in the expression, "charitable judgments." Making a charitable judgment means that *out of love for God, you strive to believe the best about others until you have facts to prove otherwise*. In other words, if you can reasonably interpret facts in two possible ways, God calls you to embrace the positive interpretation over the negative, or at least to postpone making any judgment at all until you can acquire conclusive facts.

For example, when Anne's pastor did not visit her in the hospital, she should have realized that there were at least two possible explanations. One was that he was deliberately slighting her. Another was that he had not received her note or had some other valid reason for not visiting her. If she had developed the habit of making charitable judgments, she would have believed the positive explanation until she received facts that showed otherwise.

Believing the best about others is not simply a nice thing to do; it is not an optional behavior. It is a way to imitate God himself and to show our appreciation for how he treats us. God knows everything and judges accurately. He has the final say in criticism (and in commendation). Yet he judges charitably, even mercifully, passing over and putting up with many wrongs. He is kind to ungrateful and evil people (Luke 6:35).

Charitable judgments are also an act of obedience to God. As we saw in Matthew 7:1–6, Jesus himself forbids us to judge others until we have done two things. First, we must take responsibility for any contribution we may have made to a problem. Second, we must make a diligent effort to "see clearly," that is, to accurately understand what someone else has done and why he or she did it. Therefore, whenever we gloss over our own faults, assume facts, speculate on motives, or jump to conclusions about others, we have disobeyed our Lord.

Charitable judgments are also required by Jesus' command in Matthew 7:12, where he sets forth the Golden Rule. "So in everything, do to others what you would have them do to you, for this sums up the Law and the Prophets." How do you want others to judge you? Do you want them to believe good about you instead of evil? To interpret your actions in the best possible way? To really try to understand your side of the story before drawing conclusions or talking to others about you? If so, Jesus commands that you do the same for others.

Our responsibility to judge others charitably is reinforced by Jesus' teaching on the second great commandment, "Love your neighbor as yourself" (Matt. 22:39). Just think of how quickly we judge ourselves favorably! When we are questioned or criticized, our natural response is to explain our actions in the best possible light and make excuses for any perceived wrong. If this is how we are inclined to love ourselves, it is also the way we should love others.

Charitable judgments are also implicit in the Apostle Paul's teaching on love in 1 Corinthians 13:4–7.

> Love is patient, love is kind. It does not envy, it does not boast, it is not proud. It is not rude, it is not self-seeking, it is not easily angered, it keeps no record of wrongs. Love does

not delight in evil but rejoices with the truth.
It always protects, always trusts, always hopes,
always perseveres.

Pay special attention to the last sentence:
Paul teaches that love "always protects, always
trusts, always hopes, always perseveres." In other
words, love always looks for reasonable ways to
trust others, to hope that they are doing what is
right, and to interpret their words and actions in
a way that protects their reputation and credibility. This is the essence of charitable judgments.

Notice that I said we should look for "reasonable ways" to believe the best about others.
We are not called to suspend critical thinking in
the positive sense or to make judgments that are
contrary to clear facts. If we hear someone say
something that is patently false or vicious, we
can conclude that it is wrong and legitimately
confront the speaker. But if we only hear second-
hand information or observe an act that could
be interpreted in different ways, God calls us to
withhold judgment and look for a reasonable
explanation.

The call to judge others charitably is not
something new or novel. It finds its roots in
the Ten Commandments and is consistent with
hundreds of years of church doctrine. In Exodus
20:16 God says, "You shall not give false testimony

against your neighbor." The church has historically interpreted this commandment not only to
forbid lying but also to require charitable judgments. Luther's Small Catechism teaches that this
commandment means, "We should fear and love
God so that we do not tell lies about our neighbor,
betray him, slander him, or hurt his reputation,
but defend him, speak well of him, and explain
everything in the kindest way."[2]

Similarly, the Westminster Larger Catechism
teaches that this commandment requires "pre-
serving and promoting truth between man and
man, and the good name of our neighbor, . . . a
charitable esteem of our neighbors; loving, desir-
ing, and rejoicing in their good name; sorrowing
for and covering of their infirmities; freely acknowledging of their gifts and graces, defending
their innocence; a ready receiving of a good report, and unwillingness to admit of an evil report,
concerning them. . . ."[3]

Jonathan Edwards, one of America's greatest
theologians, thoroughly discussed God's call for
charitable judgments in his superb book, *Charity and Its Fruits*.[4] Drawing on the passages dis-

---

2. Luther's Small Catechism, Question 61.

3. Westminster Larger Catechism, Question 145.

4. Jonathan Edwards, *Charity and Its Fruits:
Christian Love as Manifested in the Heart and Life*
(1852; repr., London: Banner of Truth Trust, 1962).

cussed above (Matt. 7 and 1 Cor. 13), he shows that the Bible condemns censoriousness, which he defines as "a disposition to think evil of others, or to judge evil in them," and commends charitable judgments, which he describes as "a disposition to think the best of others that the case will allow."[5]

The phrase "charitable judgments" may sound new to many of us today, but the concept itself is rooted deeply in the Word of God and the teaching of the church. Therefore, it should be rooted deeply in our hearts and displayed in our lives.

There Are Limits to Charitable Judgments

Like all principles taught in Scripture, the call to make charitable judgments does not stand against reason. It does not operate apart from other biblical commands to notice and confront wrongdoing, to protect the weak, and to promote righteousness and justice. In other words, Scripture itself teaches that there are limits to making charitable judgments.

---

5. Edwards, 204–5.

First, God's command to be charitable does not require us to believe that an action is good when there is significant evidence to the contrary. Although we should always give people the benefit of the doubt, we should not ignore clear indications that things are not as they should be. In fact, excessive charity can lead to denial and blind us to issues that need to be faced. Ignoring these symptoms only delays dealing with a problem in its early stages. This can lead to disastrous results, as David discovered when he ignored indications that Absalom was turning the people of Israel against the king (see 2 Sam. 15:1–6).

Therefore, if you see signs of a significant problem, it is appropriate to investigate the matter, ask questions, gather reliable information, and draw necessary conclusions (Prov. 18:17). If it appears that someone has done something wrong, and if that wrong is too serious to overlook (Prov. 19:11), you should go to that person and find out whether you are assessing the situation accurately (Matt. 18:15; Luke 17:3). As you approach him, you should speak tentatively instead of conclusively. For example, instead of saying, "You lied about why I was not at the meeting last night," you might say, "Perhaps I misunderstood what you said, but it sounded like you accused me of deliberately missing the meeting last night."

As you talk with the other person, you should give every opportunity for a reasonable explanation. If you did misunderstand the situation, you will have avoided needless offense. Conversely, if your concerns prove to be legitimate, God can use your loving confrontation to help the person face up to and overcome harmful actions (Gal. 6:1–2; James 5:19–20).

Second, charity does not require that we accept without question everything people tell us. Nor does it require that we naively entrust ourselves to people who do not have legitimate authority or have not proven themselves to be worthy of our trust. Since we live in a fallen world, charity must always walk hand-in-hand with discernment and wisdom (Phil. 1:9–10; James 3:14–17).

Third, the call for charitable judgments should not be used to stifle appropriate discussion, questioning, and debate. If people have sincere concerns about a matter, they should not be brushed aside with, "Just trust us." Instead, their concerns should be reasonably explored, and a genuine effort should be made to find a just and mutually agreeable solution (1 Pet. 5:2–3). At the same time, once a matter has been examined and those in authority have reached a biblically valid decision, others should respect that decision and trust that God will work through it, even if it is not the course they would have preferred (Heb. 13:17).

Finally, charity does not prevent the exercise of redemptive church discipline. When the leaders of a church believe a member is caught in a sin, they have a responsibility to seek after him, like shepherds looking for a straying sheep (Matt. 18:12–14; Gal. 6:1). If he will not repent, the church should continue to confront him lovingly and bring to bear whatever biblical discipline is necessary to help him see the seriousness of his sin and be restored to the Lord (Matt. 18:15–20).

Even these limitations on charitable judgments are to be guided by love. Whether we are believing the best about others, or discussing problems between us, our goal should always be the same: to treat them with the same charitable concern that God always shows to us.

Three Judgments to Avoid

As we seek to obey God's command to make charitable judgments, we should become alert to three ways that we judge critically. First, we think negatively of the **qualities** of others. When we develop a critical attitude toward others, we start a subtle but steady process of selective data gathering. We easily overlook or minimize others' good qualities, while at the same time we search for and magnify any unfavorable qualities. As we find faults that reinforce opinions we have already formed, we seize them eagerly, saying to ourselves (and sometimes others), "See, I told you so!" One critical judgment looks for and feeds on another, and the person's character is steadily diminished and ultimately destroyed in our minds.

The second way we judge others wrongly is to think the worst of their **words and actions**. We hear rumors of conversations or observe fragments of an opponent's behavior. Instead of searching for a favorable interpretation of their actions, or giving them a chance to explain what happened (Prov. 18:13), we prefer to put the worst construction on what they have done. We overlook things that are in the person's favor and focus on the things that seem to be against him. To top it off, we fill in the gaps with assumptions and finally judge the person to have done wrong.

One day a small church was expecting a guest preacher. He arrived early and sat in his car writing additional thoughts in his notes. He periodically put his short, white pencil in his mouth so he could free a hand to turn to a verse in his Bible. A deacon pulled in beside him, watched him for a moment, and then went inside. When the guest preacher walked into the church a few minutes later, he sensed antagonism from the entire group of deacons. He asked if he had done something wrong. The head deacon replied, "We find it very offensive that you would sit in our church parking lot smoking a cigarette, especially when you were about to preach God's Word from our pulpit!" You can imagine the deacons' embarrassment when the man pulled the pencil from his pocket and explained that he had only been working on his sermon.

The third and most insidious type of critical judgment is to assume the worst about others' **motives**. Some people are habitually cynical (distrustful or suspicious of others' nature or motives); others assume the worst only in certain people. In either case, the effect is the same: they are quick to attribute others' actions to an unworthy motive, such as pride, greed, selfishness, control, rebellion, stubbornness, or favoritism.

When doing this, they think or say things like, "All he cares about is money." "She likes to go first so she can impress everyone." "They are too proud to listen to advice." "What he really wants is to force us out of the group." "She is just too stubborn to admit she is wrong." Although these appraisals may be true on some occasions, in many cases they will be false.

So, is there ever a time that we can properly form a firm opinion about someone's motives?

Yes, we may do so whenever the other person expressly admits to such motives, or when there is a pattern of incontrovertible facts that can lead to no other reasonable conclusion.

But when such clear proof is not present, it is wrong to presume we can look into others' hearts and judge the motives for their actions. Scripture teaches that God alone can see into the heart and discern a person's motives (see 1 Sam. 16:7; Ps. 44:21; Prov. 16:2). When we believe that we also are able to do this, we are guilty of sinful presumption.

All three types of critical judgments violate God's will. Scripture sternly warns against those who indulge evil suspicions against their brothers and fail to give them a chance to explain themselves (1 Tim. 6:4; Ps. 15:3; 50:19–20). Our sin is compounded if we develop the habit of receiving or circulating evil reports about others (2 Cor. 12:20; Eph. 4:31). Jonathan Edwards likens our believing and spreading a critical judgment to "feeding on it, as carrion birds do on the worst of flesh."[6] That is what we are doing when we receive and circulate bad reports about others: it is like passing around rotting flesh.

These kinds of critical judgments also violate God's command in James 4:11–12:

---

6. Edwards, 209.

Brothers, do not slander one another. Anyone who speaks against his brother or judges him speaks against the law and judges it. When you judge the law, you are not keeping it, but sitting in judgment on it. There is only one Lawgiver and Judge, the one who is able to save and destroy. But you—who are you to judge your neighbor?

The answer to James's question is obvious. When we set ourselves up to judge critically the qualities, words, actions, or motives of others, we are doing nothing less than playing God. Just think how such behavior grieves our Lord! When we judge others in this way, we are imitating and serving the enemy of our souls. Satan is the master accuser, the father of lies, and the presumptuous judge of the saints (John 8:44; Rev. 12:10). We should be loath to do anything that imitates his ways or advances his schemes.

Critical Judgments Are Destructive and Costly

Critical judgments can do great damage to relationships and to the kingdom of God. If you assume the worst about others, you will often misjudge them and jump to conclusions. This can cause deep hurt, bring you great embarrassment, and eventually destroy relationships. A critical attitude also leads us to exaggerate others' wrongs and overlook their virtues, which distorts reality. This perspective will increasingly rob you of objectivity and often lead to decisions you later regret.

Critical judgments can also be highly contagious. Our comments influence the attitudes of those around us. Furthermore, people usually treat us as we treat them, so when we judge others harshly, it is only a matter of time before they do the same with us. Soon we are "biting and devouring each other" (Gal. 5:15).

This behavior grieves the Holy Spirit and inhibits his work in us (Eph. 4:30–32; Isa. 59:1–2). Like spiritual cholesterol in the arteries of our soul, it slows the flow of grace and can eventually lead to "heart attacks" that leave us spiritually crippled and our relationships in ruins. Critical judgments can even cripple a church. As we individual Christians judge one another critically, we undermine the unity of the church, sap its spiritual resources, and diminish its credibility and evangelistic witness to those who are watching how we treat one another (John 13:34–35).

If you critically judge others even occasionally, you will experience many of these effects. It will be far worse if you develop a habit or *disposition* to judge others critically. Scripture warns us that the longer a person indulges in negative attitudes toward others, the more habitual these attitudes become. As Psalm 109:18–19 teaches, "He wore cursing as his garment; it entered into his body like water, into his bones like oil. May it be like a cloak wrapped about him, like a belt tied forever around him" (see also Prov. 11:27; 2 Tim. 2:16). What a dreadful judgment! If you do not flee from the habit of being uncharitable, this attitude will enslave you more and more and do increasing harm to those around you.

Getting to the Root of Critical Judgments

A key step in breaking free from the habit of making critical judgments is to trace them to their source and cut them off at the root. To do this you must deal with your heart. James 4:1–12 describes two of the most common sources of critical judgments. The first is **selfishness**. When others stand in the way of what we want, we strive to remove their opposition by tearing them down and diminishing their credibility and influence in any way we can (vv. 1–3).

Pride is another source of critical judgments. Thinking that we are better than others, we set ourselves up as their judges and begin to catalog their failings and condemn their actions. As we saw earlier, when we do this we are imitating Satan by trying to play God (vv. 7, 12). Pride can also reveal itself in the inclination to believe that "I alone understand the truth about things." I think that my beliefs, convictions, theology, and doctrines are true, and I look down on anyone who disagrees with me (cf. Gal. 5:26).

Matthew 7:3–5 shows that **self-righteousness** is another root of critical judgments. When we have done something wrong but we do not want to admit it, one of the most natural things we do is to draw attention to and even magnify the failures of others.

Insecurity, which is a form of the fear of man, is a related root of this problem. When we lack confidence in our own beliefs and positions, and fear that they might be disproved, we often conclude that the best defense is a good offense. Therefore, we attack others' views and judge them before they can judge us.

Jealousy can also lead to critical judgments. As we see in Genesis 37:11, Joseph's brothers were jealous of his close relationship with God and his father, and they repeatedly interpreted his motives and actions in the worst possible way. As their jealousy grew, it culminated in their selling him into slavery.

Another cause is **self-pity**. On occasion, many of us find a perverse pleasure in feeling sorry for ourselves. Therefore, we tend to interpret situations in a way that hurts us the most. One of the best ways to do this is to interpret others' actions as a form of betrayal.

Prejudice is frequently a cause of critical judgments. When we have preconceived, unfavorable opinions about others simply because of their race, religion, gender, or status in life, we will consistently seek to validate our views by interpreting their beliefs and actions negatively.

Unforgiveness can also lead us to look for the worst in others. If someone has hurt us, and we do not forgive him, we will look for ways to justify our unforgiveness. Finding more faults in the person who hurt us is a convenient way to conceal the hardness of our own heart.

Of course, the ultimate source of critical judgments is a **lack of love**. Where love is deficient, critical judgments will be the norm. Conversely, where love abounds, charitable judgments should abound (1 Cor. 13:4–7).

Think for a moment of the wide spectrum of love you have for different people. There are probably some people in your life whom you love greatly. Usually these people have blessed you in some way. You appreciate and respect them so much that when others criticize them, you automatically think or say, "Oh, that could not be true!" No matter what they are accused of, you instinctively believe that there must be a good explanation for what they have done.

At the other end of the spectrum are people whom you love very little. They may have disappointed you, disagreed with you, hurt you, or blocked something you desired. If you are like most people, you are quick to find fault with them. You grab onto critical reports like Velcro and dismiss favorable reports like Teflon. No matter what these people do, it is difficult for you to acknowledge good in them.

What is it that separates these people in our hearts and minds? What is it that places them on the opposite ends of our rating system? Sometimes the difference arises from fundamental differences in their characters. Some people are simply more virtuous and likable than others. But in many cases the difference is found not in these other people, but in our attitudes towards them. If someone has not benefited me, agreed with me, supported me, fulfilled me, satisfied me, or otherwise demonstrated love for me, I am not inclined to love him—or to judge him charitably.

Unless God does major surgery in our hearts, these attitudes will continue to control our judgments and destroy our relationships. The good news is that *God is ready to operate.*

God Is Eager to Help Us Change

Jesus Christ came to earth to deliver us from our sins, and being judgmental is a prime sin. By dying on the cross, he purchased forgiveness and eternal life for all who believe in him (John 3:16; 6:47; 1 Pet. 3:18; 1 John 4:15).

Therefore, the first step in being delivered from this sin is to confess that you are a sinner who commits this sin. Believe that Jesus bore the punishment you deserve. Trust that his resurrection secured forgiveness and eternal life for you. Thank him for judging you with mercy rather than fairness.

Jesus does even more. He will deliver you from the sinful thoughts and behavior that plague your life and damage your relationships today (Phil. 1:6). This process is called "sanctification." It is carried out by the Holy Spirit, who works in you daily to change your heart steadily. He will help you to change your thinking, develop attitudes and habits that are pleasing to God, and make you a blessing to those around you (Phil. 2:12–13; 2 Cor. 3:18; Gal. 4:19; 5:22–26). He personally teaches us to form and express charitable judgments.

Sanctification is primarily a work of the Holy Spirit within you. It also involves your full and active cooperation. In order to grow, draw on God's grace. Strive earnestly to "put off your old self, which is being corrupted by its deceitful desires, to be made new in the attitude of your mind, and to put on the new self, created to be like God in true righteousness and holiness" (Eph. 4:22–24).

This "put off, put on" process provides the road to freedom from making critical judgments. You can begin to put off this habit by confessing your tendency to look for the worst in others and asking God to forgive you for dishonoring him, hurting other people, and weakening the witness of his church. Then you can take hold of the wonderful promise: "If we confess our sins, he is faithful and just and will forgive us our sins and purify us from all unrighteousness" (1 John 1:9).

The next step in this process is to prayerfully identify and confess the particular attitudes that feed your critical spirit. As we saw earlier, these may include selfishness, pride, self-righteousness, insecurity, jealousy, self-pity, prejudice, unforgiveness, or a lack of love. Jesus' death on the cross provides the key to putting off these sinful attitudes. When you unite yourself to Jesus through faith, he enables you to put your sinful desires to death. He also gives you power to put on the attitudes and character of Christ (Rom. 6:1–14; Col. 3:12–14).

This replacement process can be applied to each sinful attitude that leads you to judge wrongly. For example, as you ask God to help you put your pride to death, focus on and ask God to give you the humility of Jesus (Phil. 2:1–11). In the same way, ask him to help you replace self-righteousness with a greater dependence on Christ's righteousness (Rom. 1:17), insecurity with godly confidence (Phil. 4:13), self-pity with contentment (Phil. 4:12), prejudice with open-mindedness (Acts 10:27–28), unforgiveness with forgiveness (Eph. 4:32), and a lack of love with a love for others, regardless of how they treat you (Luke 23:34).

Finally, ask God specifically to help you put on the habit of charitable judging. "Father, help me to acknowledge others' virtues, delight in their successes, overlook their faults, defend their reputation, seek to understand their perspective, and believe the best about them until I have facts to prove otherwise. Help me to deal honestly, humbly, and constructively with others' true failings." As you draw on his grace and use the normal interactions of daily life to practice making charitable judgments, these attitudes and habits can become more consistent with and characteristic of the person you are becoming.

In some situations you will also need to seek forgiveness from the people whom you have misjudged. If your critical judgments have led you to treat them disrespectfully or to speak critically about them to others, you should go to them, confess your sin, and ask for their forgiveness (Prov. 28:13). True repentance will be revealed if you also go to those who heard your judgments and seek to set the record straight with them.

Another way to demonstrate repentance is to break the cycle of spreading critical reports. If someone comes to you and begins to speak critically about another person, you can promptly interrupt her and say, "Have you talked to the other person about this?" If she says no, you can respond, "Then it's not right for you to be talking about him to me or anyone else. Jesus says you should go and talk to him in private, and if that doesn't work, you can ask another believer to meet with you both to try to resolve the problem" (see Matt. 18:15–20).

Similarly, if someone speaks critically of another person or group for no constructive purpose, you can say what a friend once said to me. "I'm also concerned about what they are doing. But talking about it won't do any good. Could we pray for them right now?"

As you strive to break free from the habit of making critical judgments, it is helpful to make yourself accountable to godly people who observe your life on a daily basis. Ask them to pray for you in this area and to come talk with you when it seems you are sliding back into old habits.

As these people spur you on in your growth, some of them may even be inspired to follow your example and develop the habit of making charitable judgments themselves.

What About People Who Did Wrong in the Past?

When people have undeniably done something wrong in the past, it is difficult not to jump to the conclusion that they are doing the same thing all over again. So how can we judge them charitably? In some cases, we may be able to talk with them about their past conduct and receive assurance that they really do want to change. But such conversations are not always possible, and even when they are, we may still doubt their sincerity. What then?

Whenever we deal with someone who has done wrong in the past, we should realize that the foundation for charitable judgments is not a perfect track record, worldly optimism, or a blind hope in the fleeting goodness of man. Charitable judgments are rooted in the goodness and power of God, who promises to work graciously and unceasingly to bless his people and conform them to the likeness of his Son (Rom. 8:28–39). As Paul writes, "It is God who works in you to will and to act according to His good purpose" (Phil. 2:13). Because this is true, we can and should expect to see increasing evidences of his grace in our own lives and the lives of others.

As we embrace this truth, we can live our lives with "expectant charity." We can hope for the best in others and expect that we will eventually see God doing something good in them. But this is not to be a demanding expectation, one that has a predetermined pace and pattern. Rather it is to be a gentle expectation, one that patiently and hopefully waits for the next divinely scheduled evidence of God's work in that person's life.

For example, even though my children have repeatedly fallen short of my desires and instructions, God calls me to believe that he will be faithful to his promise to conform them steadily to the likeness of Christ. He gives me frequent opportunities to trust him in this. I recently noticed my daughter, Megan, doing something that could reasonably have been interpreted in two possible ways: as being a repeat of an old pattern (not clearing the dinner table promptly), or as being a loving act (leaving the dishes for a few minutes for a good reason). Faith in God's transforming promises enabled me to withhold my critical judgment and hope for the best. Moments later I discovered that Megan had been helping her grandmother get something out of her closet. How grateful I was that I had not jumped to a critical conclusion when my daughter was doing an act of love.

We have a powerful motivation for making charitable judgments—even of those who have done wrong in the past. It is the desire to honor God by imitating his mercy and kindness toward us (Eph. 5:1; Luke 6:36). Because of our past sins, God has every right to judge us with lethal and eternal criticism. Yet he is merciful, kind, patient, and gracious. He does not treat us as our sins deserve, and he always looks for the best in us (Ps. 130:3). If that is how he treats us, then we should be eager to honor him by doing the same with others (see also Rom. 12:9; Col. 3:12–13; 1 Pet. 4:8).

So, if you struggle with a critical spirit, remember the goodness of God and his power to change people. Cultivate a desire to bring him praise by imitating his mercy and kindness to you. As you do so, you will find it increasingly natural to release people from their previous wrongs and judge their behavior today with the charity of Christ.

A Living Example

Carl is a living example of a man who has cultivated the habit of making charitable judgments. Although he is a long-time friend and we agree on most things, we have occasionally disagreed on significant issues. Yet I have always felt completely free to speak frankly about my opinions, even when it is apparent that Carl holds a very different view. Why? I think it is because I have never once felt judged or condemned by Carl. Even when he thinks I hold a wrong view or am guilty of sin, he has never said a word, used a tone of voice, or given me a look that indicates he condemns me or thinks less of me.

On the contrary, I always feel that he makes an earnest effort to understand my views, to find any legitimacy in them, and to reexamine his own beliefs in the light of our disagreement. Even when he has confronted me about my sin, I have felt a pervading sense of love and encouragement, not condemnation. And more than once I have heard that he gave me the benefit of the doubt when others spoke ill of me. Nor does he limit his charity to me. Even when I judge or speak critically of others to Carl, he refuses to play the game, even if that person has made his life difficult.

Carl treats others with a remarkable uniformity. Whether people treat him well or poorly, whether they agree with him or not, whether they advance his goals or block them, he has a habit of believing the best about them and resisting the temptation to find fault in them. Instead of breathing judgment, like some people I know, Carl continually breathes grace. As a result, people are drawn to him. They feel safe sharing their opinions, questions, and weaknesses around him, without fear of being judged. As Carl looks for the best in people, many of them (including me) are inspired to live up to his charitable opinion of them. As a result, the more time people spend with him, the more they grow in faith and character.

By God's grace, Carl is imitating the charitable attitude of our Lord Jesus Christ. When Jesus spoke with the Samaritan woman at Jacob's well, she was drawn to him (John 4). Although she was guilty of great sin, she felt safe in his presence and did not fear condemnation. Jesus looked for the best in her, and she was inspired to change. As a result, she brought glory to God.

This is the effect I would like to have on people around me. I'm sure you would also. If God can enable Carl to imitate Jesus by making charitable judgments, he can do it for us. Starting today, let's ask him to inspire us and enable us always to believe the best about others until we have facts to prove otherwise.

Help Me to Judge Rightly

Lord, help me to judge others
    as I want them to judge me:
Charitably, not critically,
Privately, not publicly,
Gently, not harshly,
In humility, not pride.

Help me to believe the best about others
    until facts prove otherwise—
To assume nothing,
    to seek all sides of the story,
And to judge no one until I've removed
    the log from my own eye.

May I never bring only the Law,
    to find fault and condemn.
Help me always to bring the Gospel,
    to give hope and deliverance,
As you, my Judge and Friend,
    have so graciously done for me.

Contributors

David V. Edling, series editor, is a retired Coast Guard captain who served on active duty for ten years and twenty more in reserve service.

Gary Friesen is an attorney and serves as the executive vice president of Peacemaker Ministries, overseeing the day-to-day ministry activities of this growing international organization.

The Rev. Alfred Poirier is senior pastor of Rocky Mountain Community Church, Billings, Montana. Rev. Poirier serves as the chairman of the board of directors of Peacemaker Ministries, is a Certified Christian Conciliator of the Institute for Christian Conciliation, and also teaches as an adjunct instructor for Peacemaker Ministries.

Ken Sande, an attorney, is the president of Peacemaker Ministries and the author of *The Peacemaker*, *Peacemaking for Families*, and numerous articles on the application of God's word to conflict.